Advance Praise

"Home is the structure you build when nowhere else will have you," writes Ann Tweedy in this gutsy, no-nonsense collection of poems built on a precarious and often tender journey through homes no longer available to return to. The result is neither sadness nor nostalgia; it is hard, clean narrative of self-preservation and survival, fitted with unexpected joy. I feel such kinship with these poems, their testament to the strength and determination of women and men who struggle to build life anew, and to find home and happiness in a world of travail. What a blessed space this book is: a home for the wayward soul.
* D. A. Powell, American Poet *

Ann Tweedy's first book is a brave and honest examination of liminality. In delicate lyrics she confesses to trespass, asking readers to question the boundaries between acts and identity, sexuality and family. *The Body's Alphabet* documents the poet's courage, living openly as a bisexual feminist. Although childhood logic taught her that "home is the structure / you build when nowhere else will have you," these beautiful poems knit and nest safe haven for a life spent gathering freedom.
* Carol Guess, author of *Doll Studies: Forensics* *

What made me sit down and read *The Body's Alphabet,* cover to cover, in a single evening? Perhaps it is the way that I know, in Ann Tweedy's poems, I will find the unvarnished truth, and a voice with "the drowsed freedom to talk about anything." And I know I will find that truth compassionately rendered, details delicately arranged like the flowers of the "dutiful and stubborn" forsythia of which she writes. This is a book about finding homes for ourselves—homes for our adult selves, even as complex memories of our childhood homes still live inside us; homes for our bodies; homes in the natural world. Tweedy's vision is both hopeful and wise.
* Katrina Vandenberg, author of *Atlas* and *The Alphabet Not Unlike the World* *

The

Body's

Alphabet

*

The Body's Alphabet

*

Ann Tweedy

Headmistress Press

ISBN-13: 978-0692613825
ISBN-10: 069261382X

Cover art © Self-Portrait 1906, Imogen Cunningham Trust
Cover & book design by Mary Meriam

P U B L I S H E R

Headmistress Press
60 Shipview Lane
Sequim, WA 98382
Telephone: 917-428-8312
Email: headmistresspress@gmail.com
Website: headmistresspress.blogspot.com

For R.A.F.T.

And in memory of D.P.M.

Contents

dirt-blurred

falling and alighting

Some of the religious say the five senses are thieves
so let's say I am stolen

—Linda Hogan, from "Eucalyptus"

unguarded

Eggshells

because i lived for 18 years
with a hallway carpet of scattered
newspaper, with junkmail piles on the ironing
board, the kitchen table, the counter,
with holes in the rotting floor
that my mother dug deeper
when she got bored, i tread through
the world mindful that upsets
follow unguarded movement.

others translate my cautious
gait, the space i don't
take up, into weakness and fear.
their sure-footed strides
haven't yet tripped them—
their careless gestures have not set off
a single avalanche. they know no vigilance,
having never trudged through war.

half-life

home for the yearly visit in february
i sit with you in the rented car in the dirt
driveway that threads from one end
of the lot to the other. already
the house is so near to falling
down that you won't let me in
and you won't leave the half-acre yard for fear
that someone will break in. somewhere

beyond a daughter's jurisdiction, doctors
weave scientific labels through
the spokes of mystery. if i could read
about my mother in words indifferent as steel
instruments, would i feel more or less that i exist?

so far, the only names i know belong to the ones
you blame. *Chris Barns is writing a book about me—if he*
calls you tell me. i get $1,000 for every privacy
violation. i know you've talked to Mark Kraus; didn't
he call you yesterday? Harold Johns put him up
to trying to take my house away. do you know what terror is?

imagine waking up near 30 to realize
your mother has always been insane.
if you could reclaim the psyche, what
colors would you shade perception in?

the pictures i like best are black and whites
of a dark-haired girl in a pale dress. girl

with a doll, girl with a puppy. maryjanes with white socks
and a background of grass. her face turned slightly,
the girl half-smiles at the camera. it's that mixture
of willingness and caution i believed in

fracture

mom, if i could, i'd erase the house
with its piles of newspaper   unopened
mail   old shoes   do you believe
me   this is the little girl that never
lied telling you   i'd take away the neighbors
who surveyed their yard to stake out boundaries
from you   the kids who rode too close
on bicycles as you walked home   they chanted
insults my mind won't remember—*witch* or *hag* or *welfare
mother* or *crazy broken out of work*
i'd take away the voices that only
know how to hurt   also the chemicals
that ruined your system   made you think
everyone was poisoning you   oh
if i could go back that far   before
i was born when you lived in another state
and worked for chemical companies   smart
female college graduate fighting for a job
in places that would ruin you
i'd take away the chemicals and the need
to fight too   even your mother, who cried
on the corner when she learned
she was pregnant with you   your sister
consoling her   where do i go from here?
the brother who molested you   whose side
your mother took in arguments   the puppets
who enact scripts from your scarred
interior, like the projections Jung imagined
everyone making except that they are all malevolent:

they're stealing your house   your tranquilizer
prescriptions   your vitamins
they unlock doors with illegal keys
while you sleep, brazen in the charged
minutes after the physical body
overpowers the will   and what would be left
if the daughter, the selfish only child, worked
miracles, mom, what would be left of you?

Interior Architecture

It's almost meaningless to say the house was bulldozed,
that house with its pale yellow clapboard exterior, deceptive
    somehow.
White shutters with red shapes, rotting window boxes.
It was a place that a child could not invite friends to,
it was a prison of artificial walls, the stacks of newspapers, old mail,
    the boxes
of who knows what, the careful stepping of the child through those
    rooms.
The child didn't notice the careful steps, how they became part of
    her.
This is not surprising, this is how learning happens, without
    noticing.
The crowding happens that way too, slowly. It feels worse
when someone else sees it, like the man fixing the furnace
looking at the girl, now ten, and she at him, wordlessly.
And she imagined pity, but those were her own thoughts talking.
What passed between them was clear-eyed, steady, indecipherable.

It was decades later that the house was bulldozed
by the buyer of the land, after the tax foreclosure. There are likely
    records
to prove it, permits and the bills of a contractor, filed somewhere.
One can even drive by where the house used to be and see a better
    house,
the yard almost filled with its oversized footprint. It's nicer,
the father of the little girl says to his grown up daughter,
and the pleasure that tinges his sentence estranges her.

But the house is inside the child and the grown up woman. She sits
        in the study
of her new house in another state and feels the old house in her.
Looking out the window at night, the streetlight a few yards off
evokes it, the dirt driveway with its long, narrow swath of yard on the
        other side.
She remembers her mother telling her about watching the bulldozer,
        how the new owner
threatened to call the police if she touched her piles of stuff, now
        littering the yard,
while neighbors sifted. The daughter knows her own stuff was in
        there too and that all of this is true,
but the house still frames her eyes, those crumbling shutters.
Looking out of her window at night, she feels herself within it.
She still walks carefully, without thinking about it.
What is it that loss takes from us?

pale pink

the forsythia were not beautiful
but dutiful and stubborn, predictable like little else—
two sentries of the driveway that no one trimmed,
so that their woody fingers would scrape a car
on either side, should one venture in. and the small lilacs
growing out of pine needle dirt didn't blossom,
yet i couldn't help my affection for them. the efforts
that don't succeed, the days we just get by, shouldn't we
love them? only the roses in their ballet splendor
seemed out of place among that chaotic, undernourished flora.
they grew for a few feet
along rotting poles and rails. nobody did anything
for them. they weren't particularly healthy or robust. but every year:
flowers—each with a few tender layers and a tangle of tan
pollen-laden anthers. i'd inhale their rich, delicate perfume
and think back to the unknown family
who owned the house before us. who knows what possessed them
or even what state they left in, but i could close my eyes and almost
        conjure
the yard they must've dreamed of.

thresholds

paean for the body

achy, sore, content, energized, strong, weak,
worn out, too big or too small, caged—
jammed in too tight denim or afloat in clothes
that once fit. perched on wiggly jiggly
high heels or braced squarely by boots.
pinched, prodded, evaluated,
sized up, found wanting or passable,
given a clean bill or admitted to the hospital.

she's a chip we can cash in if we need to,
before the expiration date when she's removed
from the shelf of desirables. exploiting her
through paid sex, married sex, stripping, or cocktail
waitressing are all ways to make a living.
she could be the ugly girl next door
or the kid brother you resented having to take care of.

often, she's the one we know best and like least,
having counted the grey hairs, glared at the moustache,
applied cream to the wrinkles, glowered at the flesh
spilling over the waistband, mourned the nose's tilt
or the way one eye's smaller than the other,
especially when tired. we think the messages
we send her go nowhere, like letters
children mail to santa claus or expletives
flung at the tv. we only wish she'd listen
and want less or want more, not grumble about
hunger or exercise, stop saving those fat cells
for the lean days our brains don't anticipate, try

harder to build muscle. if we eat sweets without
sugar or fat she can't process, we might
outsmart her. the funny thing we know
without knowing is that
really there's nothing but her—
to say we need her doesn't quite capture it—
so of course she hears everything.

appointment

the hairdresser's fingers massaging
shampoo into my scalp feel
so much like an intimate caress
that in sixth grade i told my best friend
i didn't like to have my hair cut   back when
my body was getting ready to cross many
thresholds, it seemed wrong to pay someone
to do something so enjoyable   now that i openly crave
a woman's touch, i like the process
as much as the inkling of newness you leave with

first the fingers work the shampoo
while you recline against a sink with a neck-shaped dip:
hot water and wiry muscles and always
an expensive aroma like peppermint or a delicate
fruit. then there is the drowsed freedom
to talk about anything

the last time i saw lisa, my hairdresser
in california, she was getting
a divorce and i was graduating law school.
i remember her dark, medium length hair, her flashy
boutique clothes, her barely noticeable limp.
she'd always seemed happy and this time
told me how she liked living alone
with her cat and being in a city,
close to everything. still, she felt bad
that joel wanted to work it out and she
couldn't anymore. her hands sectioned off

my hair, snipping the usual masterpiece. she wanted
to give him the house and most everything
else but her lawyer kept pushing for more. i sat
in the rotating chair facing the mirror; words
filtered through a blur of worried ecstasy.

The Full Pulse of Happiness

when i was in elementary school,
i watched girls and guys gather
in big old impalas and cutlasses
in the dirt lot behind george's cleaners.
back then the prettiest girls in the world
worked as cashiers at the supermarket—
but the rest of them were here

walking home from the grocery,
the five and dime, the train station,
after dark my mother and i would see them:
sitting in cars parked close
together, smoking, eating donuts,
drinking beer. the girls wore
tight designer jeans and spaghetti
strap tank tops. now and then, they'd ride
down north main with their boyfriends,
streaking on lipstick and shadow, brushing
swaths of permed hair. my mother thought
it was impolite for a girl to groom
in front of her boyfriend, but i doubted
politeness could get you anywhere

sometimes the mother of a kid that lived
near my babysitter was there, and sometimes
the kid too. she was a year or so younger
than me. the mother sat in a car
while the kid stood outside drinking soda
or eating packaged ice cream. an open car window

siphoned the mother's crimped voice:
tara, get over here. still, i couldn't help
but envy the girl—she got to watch
and, if that wasn't enough, they bought her
all the bite-sized pleasures a kid could bear

A Bargain

I peed the bed to comfort
myself when I was little. Warmth and
a familiar, acrid smell—
a surrounding
of self with self.
But the embrace

faded into shivers. Why didn't
I become a criminal
with all the other bed wetters?
She's still inside me. I ply
her with chocolate to stop her.

Small Town Vignettes

if i try to go back there
my soul resists
but i can tell you this:
girls in shorts as spring nears summer
trying to showoff their legs and thighs
because what else is there?
in school the desks said things like
i blew eddy and he was 12 inches
yum yum yum yum.

or i could tell you about churches:
the little brown one that my mother
got kicked out of for talking badly
of a fellow parishioner.
she thought the other's trained hymnsinging
overdramatic with its trills and tras

she was arrested twice on the steps
and then convicted
once for trying to get in. it didn't have
beautiful stained glass like the white
congregational perched on the common

and the minister was from texas not one
of the beloved local boys everyone remembers
shoveling driveways or winning fieldgoals
on thanksgiving. and it wasn't st. mary's
that you had to be popular to go to
but it made the news and my fifth grade year miserable.

or i could tell you about my paper route
in seventh grade—the gang of boys that said *die
dog bitch,* playing some kind of ball game
in the street. i wondered coldly if they would kill
or rape me for the endless minutes that one of them
stood in front of me. but the texture couldn't be wrought

without the insinuating dss woman: *Your mother
never answered the door but we could hear
footsteps inside* and i wondered how
that was a crime but in her language—
in front of a judge—
it meant *hiding something hiding something,*

or the hum of airplanes from the municipal
airport that continuously permeated
our house. they didn't carry unobtainable
dreams like commercial jets
of places and distances. they were flown
by private people mostly probably
born with money and so i never dreamed
of being in one bound for some other place—
still their hum and buzz are the sound
of home however little sought after
that sometimes is

a few remaining trees

when i cross the country to visit, my father squeezes meeting me
into shopping trips and work appointments
so his wife won't know he breaches her order
to steer clear of the daughter
who won't keep quiet. and i can't deny it hurts
to skulk among aisles with my father
instead of chatting on his couch or driving to visit grandma.

yet, even a sham errand shelters the joy
of being two or three and riding aloft his shoulders
at the Fourth of July parade.
there was the thrill of seeing everything for a me
normally lost amid grown-up legs
and the pride of being held high. that moment inhabits
us like a ladyslipper
among a few remaining trees.

terror

my old friend, haven't you stood with me
at every turn of my life, like a parent
urging and impeding
each step, saying *you can't, you must*
so that when i went, i would sometimes—maybe often—
fail, believing *you can't* but driven by
you must, my ambition a fever that carries me
beyond happiness, beyond comfort, always
to the next discovery. but i have loved you
all this time, though for many years
i wouldn't have admitted it. how could i not love
obstacles that drive me on and on—
places i never would have thought to go
except i saw a barrier pretending to stop me, and haven't you been
the greatest among them?

to stand in the face of you and make you
watch me do the thing you've told me not to!
it's not success or failure anymore—it's just doing,
saying *no* and *yes* to you at once. it's not that you don't
make me fumble, it's that i keep going
despite that, feeling the rush of walking with you.
i call on you now—as i stand on the precipice
of pregnancy. of course you're here already, were here before it
      came
to this, saying *no yes.* i let myself believe *no* for as long
as i could, but at last i've come to challenge you.

Rupture

Each contraction transformed me
into sky rived by lightning,
nature's impossible violence
incarnate in every shockwave.
The human was lost then
in the animal, but terror,
my erstwhile companion, was gone too.
Odd in those moments of cleaving to find it
swallowed by walls
of animal pain and animal effort.

the pharmacy

M. with his quick eyes
examining the maxi pads
looking for the thickest ones
to soak in witch hazel and freeze
for me. the clerk saying
can i help you with something?
M. explaining that his wife
just had a baby. me waiting at home,
mostly bed-ridden, recipient
of so many blessings

beholden

he exited my body and immediately knew
what he wanted to do. one nipple cracked and bled.
the other became tender as sunburn.
he took hour-long breaks,
but it felt constant to me. in the hospital,
lactation specialists hovered, offered nipple protectors,
hydrogel pads, recommended formula supplements, rest
for my damaged breast. i slathered on wool wax,
ruined shirts with nipple-range
grease spots.

months later, when skin began to heal, his mouth
became a strange tickle.

once in those early months, i took a plane cross country
and stowed my pump in checked baggage. before the flight was done,
my breasts had become baseballs,
ached like they might explode. i remember pained small talk
with the taxi driver en route to the hotel, squelching tears
during check in.

somewhere around six months, he started to toy with me,
pulling and turning one nipple while he sucked the other.

at eight months, he screamed at the ensconcing
of the nursing cover. i became a reluctant
exhibitionist. men in restaurants stared. a woman
glared unabashedly. now he's almost three.

i unsnap my bra, push him on, and try not to see myself
from others' eyes. to some, i'm all body,
exactly what i never wanted to be.

he strokes my unused breast like a lover,
kneads my belly contemplatively.
his fingers search out the left side's mole,
which he rubs like a rabbit's foot.

sometimes i try to stop him. others, i wonder
if i'll ever be loved this much again.

between planets

taking stock

last year, the lebanese
palm reader pictured domestic
peace, a single union, in our separate,
unscarred hands. now, godless
and short on faith, i recall the howl
of sirens four years previous, when our packed
u-haul accelerated downhill
from a gas station in crook county,
wyoming. neither of us was sure
about moving cross-country but you were
less sure than me. when two cops
arrested you for a suspended license
i managed not to scream.

we had to get to san francisco
for your interview, so i forced an absurd smile
when the lead cop said, *we don't take*
triple A bail bonds, travelers checks
or credit cards. today's saturday. if she can't
post bail, we'll haul you 200 miles
to sundance and let them sort it out on monday

at the corner store, in line for the cashier,
i remembered how the clerks in mansfield,
massachusetts would stare
or ignore me, the crazy
woman's daughter. for a self left
to the goodwill of strangers,
i felt a welling of disdain.

still, i sucked that dusty air
down to my diaphragm and said
my husband's in jail—will you cash these in?

zing

when you catch someone's eye
and feel the zing of attraction,
isn't it strange how your surroundings
get sucked into a void around you?
it's as if the spotlight's on you
and that person—all other lights
have been dimmed. i remember the man
who worked at the gourmet burrito shop
when i was in law school. Ángel was his name.
i'd listen to the mexican women
who worked there say it. *Ángel.* twined
in their mouths, i thought i'd never heard a word
so beautiful, couldn't believe
that was his name. but there it was—
in their mouths, on his name tag.

my husband and i would go in.
he'd say our order and Ángel and i
would stare at each other. in the stream
of that looking, i felt intensely alive, as if
i'd stepped into light-filled paradise.
the sounds of customers chatting,
the banter of employees, a garble
as if underwater. but once
i went back to the counter
after having sat down with my husband—
something was missing, maybe sauce
or a drink, and i wanted to ask Ángel

for it, even in the impersonal manner
of restaurant service. wrapped
in co-workers' watch out looks,
he measured each word, as if to keep it from talking.

maybe i was too dangerous alone,
my husband in a chair a few feet away.
or maybe you can't seek out
that melting, that magic wardrobe. you have to find it
without looking. it just has to come.

word games

3 newspapers: *the guardian, the willamette week, the stranger*
to you i owe my life as i know it, in other words some homage,
3 cups of regret, a little too much turbulence from the
egg beater, or the electric mixer, as the more well off say,
did i say *regret?* i didn't mean it, in fact i've never
believed in it, at least not since high school when i decided
if you could live your life over, you'd make the same mistakes,
they'd just be more frustrating. but i was telling
you about newspapers, the personal ads i mean
and the classifieds. from *the guardian* i got nude
photography jobs and men to do threesomes along with my husband,
from *the willamette week* i got female lovers, from the
stranger i got a girlfriend, a companion, whose love
scares my husband. this is stream of consciousness—it isn't real—
some words just sound better following other words. like *love*
should always follow a word like *girlfriend*—*husband* often
works too. *husband* and *girlfriend* aren't conventionally understood
to go well together, though most people worry about it happening
the other way around, as in *husband who has a girlfriend*
which is certainly common enough to worry about. but others
take words like puzzle pieces and try to fit them together
when they don't really go, thinking they're artists or trailblazers,
that originality has its own reward and god i mean
it better because it's only grief when you look at external
consequences: *husband, girlfriend* and *female lover.*
i'm telling you those 3 newspapers are a dangerous combination—
no holds barred—you can find whatever you want in them
things you didn't know you wanted till you saw the listing,
but don't think, after you pick up the phone, you can climb

back into the little box of your life. you could end up
like me: words from a magnetic poetry set, *husband*
and *girlfriend,* spending your time trying to do something with them.

Outing

it has become almost religious: two or three times
each week, i drive an hour to see women pretend
they are men. their breasts have been wound
and flattened, their hair cut short, they are
equipped with penises of duct tape and sock.
in cowboy hats and jeans, white shirts and ties,
they lip sync in an alphabet only the body can interpret

and what of the body, who for thirty years staked
her allegiance in one nation, while admitting to break
its lesser edicts about sex and love,
who and how many? imagine that self-proclaimed outlaw
dreaming a life of prescribed normalcy

i see myself now, for six months caught between planets:
loving a man i mean to spend my days with and a woman
who dances on-stage for anyone who can afford
cover. her repertoire of male voices, from pop
to country, thrills because of an underlying forgery

do you think i could write myself back into
the hewn dimensions of any single space? home is the structure
you build when nowhere else will have you

If

if you offered me earnestly the saliva-
tinged notes i have savored
in passing, during
the numbers when i am among
the women who tip you
and kissing me
looks good on-stage: femme
to your butch   train to your
station   wave to your
ocean   wind to your cave

if you impressed on me—for as long
as a minute—the lips you have
meted out like a parent, moist
pressure to the cheek
on odd tuesdays, every
few weeks, the split-second
press of tongue on the belly,

if you took my thick
ruddy wings, ragged from the gouge
of incisors, into your own
like a blessing, and then
separated them
with a poke of budded muscle

there would open a
trapdoor to heaven.
in the gardens

underneath, the rarest
blooms would begin
their brief seasons

dirt under the fingernails

the women who loved me
occupy my past. you can take
a tourist train to visit
the fights and the tears,
the put-downs and the barren
silences, replayed over and over
because suffering,
like moxie, makes you stronger,
because there's no point is there
in nostalgia, because nothing
can be gained by chasing after
yesterday, so you may as well slather
the beauty and the warmth, the orgasm
on the boulder in the middle of the river,
with the black paint of despair.

in my present, the secret little voice
says i'm nothing without them,
yes listen again—*no-thing   with-out   them,*
none of their friends will want
to talk to me now. their leaving
proves i can't be loved.
there's not much to say back.
married, bisexual, i am dirt under the finger-
nails of both communities: speck
of black that greys the perfect
white of straightness, speck of white
that greys the perfect black of queerness.
oversexed, non-monogamous bi woman,

i *could* choose but won't.

oh part of me is proud—
that *won't* says something for all of us,
says we can make our picks *regardless* of the other options,
says it's all up to me, the individual.

and yet.

Home Remedies

on my worst days i empathize
with murderous husbands from the forensic
tv show. beneath most killings festers
commonplace unhappiness: not enough
money, a pending divorce, an affair
on one side or the other. some things
are new; everything else
takes pains to be old.

at first i'd dream
the husband i've loved
for 16 years
might disappear miraculously
through no fault of my own.
poof. what easier segue
to *lesbian* could there be?
and then i could grieve
properly.

but now i see myself slipping
into the whirlpool
to disappear down the drain.
on tv, knives, bullets,
shoelace beckon.
in death, is any solace
greater than a loved one's
ministration? i picture my shining
dance into nothingness.

why won't he kill me?

mainland fantasy

somewhere there's a sandy island
with a few palm trees   if i could
subsist on coconuts   only
lizards would talk to me
i'd earn their willingness
using insects and plant matter

though in weather that single-minded
and dazzling   plants could
flourish only in shady pockets
and befriending lizards would go slowly.
still my problems might begin to make sense
inside a cage of brightness

eventually i think i'd mourn
the monotony of coconuts   the reluctance
of lizards   who have better things
to do than befriend a love-starved human,
but here in seattle's dark winter rain

i'm dreaming of their thick pleated
skin   of black blinking
eyes with no flash of recognition
i'm imagining an end to stubborn expectation
to the ego's striving to fit in

life without descartes

if you could look at love and see
love and not   a struggle against hate

if you could rejoice in the unruly
fusion of fat, muscle, and bone
every day those water-gorged roses
shine out   of the skin and the eyes

open   if the intellect were proud
to be as practical as a board
and a nail   a way to eat   if

you named all the parts of yourself
whole, beautiful: the darkness
and the light need each other
you never   have to choose

Praise

"Ever newly begin the praise you cannot accomplish."
—Rilke, from "The First Elegy"

I praise my belly's first hunger pains as I sit here upstairs
reading and typing so that my ears begin to strain
among words for cooking sounds and movement sounds,
the sounds of being taken care of. I praise the faucet
when the water finally begins to run, that flutter
that inundates me for a moment, knowing as I do
the cooking has begun. I praise the gentle bang
of cabinet doors and the muted thud of the refrigerator
opening, then closing against the cushion of its rubber lip.
I praise the grocery shopping he does, examining
my wishes in his mind, then implementing them like a building plan.
I praise his perusal of all-natural frozen meals
for those that don't have chicken and aren't too fatty, searching out
especially the exotic and the new. I praise the cage-free eggs he buys
so that I won't be part of tiny cages
full of chickens that can't stand up, feathers furling
out the roof-holes. I praise the cat box he scoops
to save me from gagging. I praise his trips for moisturizer, birdseed.
I praise the laundry he does, tireless
after a long day of work, the desire for some kind of order,
though washed, unfolded clothes lie strewn
about the house. I praise the hands
that sometimes are too eager and wash a dry-clean-only skirt or tumble
a line-dry pair of pants. I praise the flashes of anger
that overtake me then. I praise the minutes he saves me each day
so that I can tell you how it is, knowing
I could say anything.

kilter

when the days line up flat
one after another ahead of me
and i feel like a traveling salesman
whose territory is the wide, plowed,
sectioned-off midwest: contiguous squares
and rectangles chopped into rows
and columns, as orderly as abacuses,
never off-kilter for even a minute,

thinking of your body saves me.
i think of how we fit together—
your slopes and my angles
irregular, messy perfection.
i think of your oblong breasts,
the left smaller than the right,
how your resistant nipples harden
finally between my rubbing fingers
or against the insistent
beat of my tongue—taut moments when
my body understands rhythm
and teases and trains your pleasure
to the song that we're writing together

i think of the faint acrid smell of your smooth
slightly tan skin, the smell that clings to the strands
of your armpit hair, strongest when I rest my head
half against your large upper arm and half
against your chest, of how resting there

both stirs me and puts me at ease—sensations
the female body alone can synchronize.

i think of the way, sitting up, you examine
my body lying on the bed, marveled
by my collarbone or the new
leaves of shoulder muscle or the jut
of my pelvis like the current-scoured
stone you palmed before we met. and i remember
how your eyes drink me with the slow lap
of an animal accustomed to abundance,
your eyes that look and look
and still each morning
see me new, and then all the coming hours
begin to breathe that promise too.

Porous Landscape

"There's a particular hold love has over you when you're afraid of who you love."
—Mark Doty

i.
i was trapped in van gogh's
painting of the starry night,
except it wasn't just the light
swirling—every part of the landscape
was engaged in a terrible flux.
lacking church and houses,
my vista was trees, grass and
spiraled clouds. the moon
was my girlfriend's
face, laughing. as i walked,
the ground shifted and rose up
and would have grabbed
me had i not, at the last moment, jumped.

ii.
fear tightens love's hold
on the lover. love makes fear
crave more of itself. i awoke
from my dream and gasped with
horror. i awoke and understood
that i lived in the dream
painting with my lover but
lay there thinking and decided
not to tell her. i awoke
and wanted to walk that
porous landscape forever.

stain

at christian camp, aged 14,
i remember the counselor explaining—
wherever a guy touches you, it's like ink
staining you. it never goes away.
the other campers and i gazed at our pretty, straight-
haired counselor and nodded, struck
by our potential for sin.

no one mentioned being touched by other women then,
but now that you're gone and the memory
of your hands on my body—
though replayed almost hourly—
blurs, i wonder about that ink
threatened–or promised–so long ago.
shouldn't it be, like any threat of punishment
taken in and stored, mine for eternity?
it must be invisible—residue of joy
in the cells of the nipples you'd skim
then suck, dream-tinges along my waist's
inlets where your hands cinched
as we danced, deep smolder
that simmers from hours when–
fingers or silicone, rough or tender—
i was always happy, taken up
with the pleasures of giving.
but, as i imagine a future
fraught with missing you, i wish the ink blared
so i could point to it and say *see, see how we loved*
each other? look at the enormous indigo birthmark

i'll always carry for her, like the flame in a monument
that never goes out.

now i know those tattoos
of lovers' names aren't born
of a foolish belief in permanence
but of a kind of quixotic hope.

near the entrance of Madison Market

when i saw you in the co-op
grocery, woman i have missed
these months since our break up,
my legs decided that they
were in a race, while my mind
contrived to get your
attention. but when your eyes
at last caught mine, my larynx choked
"hey" as my long legs rushed
me past you. i witnessed your mouth
opening and registered your light-
filled eyes pulling at my insides
with an insistence that said
i would let myself be yours
again. but, safe in the stocked
aisles, i swallowed the irony
of being—finally—whom you'd wanted
all along: a woman so afraid of love
she'll bolt toward a stack of sale-priced noodles.

bulkheads

1.
what kind of memory does the band-tailed
pigeon have that it fears us
because, years ago, we hunted it?
great blue herons were also hunted,
but they look you in the eye,
face-to-face, until you come within a few feet—
then they squawk and row slowly away
to show they don't think much of you.
bald eagles, too, look straight at you.
they could care less if you mean
well or have a gun—they know
how little we amount to and are willing
to risk telling us. if one's ever
peered at you from a tree limb,
looking down its hooked beak the way
a disgruntled judge might consider you over the ridge
of her reading glasses, you know what i mean.

2.
lately, there's not much i'm willing
to risk telling you. the other day, when i called
to find out how your dog was after hearing
he'd been attacked by the neighbor's mutt,
i wanted to hang up as soon as i heard
"hello." i felt like a kid who screws up
her courage to open the closet door
and check for monsters, only to scream

and slam it shut before her eyes
can adjust to darkness.

it's not the well-meant betrayals i'm afraid of—
how for months you hid
your growing dissatisfaction and pain
behind a wall of smiles
or how you cooked me dinner just before
breaking it off, trying to replicate
the meal we'd shared in Morocco
down to the ceramic platter you'd bought there,
so that, for the rest of the night,
i tried to retch that tomatoey hamburger up.

the danger is feeling the love
i still have for you. i keep it
locked down tight. when it starts to rise,
i gasp from the crushing cube of pain
in the middle of my chest. it takes all my muscle
to push the love back down again,
to make it lie, drugged, along my diaphragm,
instead of delivering its paralyzing venom
to every extremity.

3.
i'm with the pigeons. pride and bravado
have no place here. little can be gained
from even the boldest emotional
fuck you, but the losses are incalculable.

somersault

when you left me, i went back
to being me again, which was a hell of a lot
simpler than having been some new me
loved by you. then, i'd been
the envy of practically every woman
in seattle, most of whom wanted either to be with
or to be you. to myself, i'd had a lot
of explaining to do. how could i,
this shy married girl, new to loving
women, have snagged you? was happiness
on a timer, just waiting to run out?
and when exactly would sadness be fully
cooked and ready to remove from the oven?

daily, i worked at believing none of this
was true. you were evidence that the world
didn't work the way i'd thought. painstakingly,
i tried to rewrite my history
to accommodate you. the person i could barely
love myself was loved by you. i could almost
overlook your shifts in warmth (due, i'd learn
later, to the husband in the foreground)
because affection itself was a nearly blinding
revelation. like a dazzled viewer
of da vinci's *last supper,* beauty
derailed my ability to register the cracks

in our paint. but the old history stayed legible
under my determined cross-outs. like a once-popular

religion, it believed in itself. and waited for me,
knowing my will to disown it would be only temporary.

fungus

athlete's foot! the dermatologist pronounces
when I show him my dry flaky heel and describe
the little red bumps that sometimes surface
along the rim. when i protest that it's lasted
a couple of years, intermittently, having resisted
creams and powders, he retorts
i've had mine since vietnam, which forces me
to see, in the dried up, sober doctor,
a young soldier, sweating in the trenches
while his choppered squad leader
determines maneuvers. after that, i try to like him.

athlete's foot! i go home and contemplate
ways to tell my girlfriend. the ringworm—
red half-dollar itching, swelling
from my shoulder—is somehow easier
being temporary and probably transmitted
by her kittens. at night, our feet bump
under the covers and i cringe at
my sin of omission.

a few months later, the doctor goes too far—
ranting that lawyers are destroying the health
profession, exclaiming about my acne–the pimple
of my last visit an "impressive"
stage four—as if it's the worst case
he's seen, but refusing to prescribe
medicine because i might sue him.
i realize—vietnam or no vietnam—
i don't like him. and i go off

to find a new doctor. months later,
the girlfriend will leave me—
thirty years into her future,
even a fungoid foot
won't call up my memory.

dirt-blurred

fruit

think of how the body labors—
day in, day out, it does its difficult work.
take, for instance, the man who tucked himself
against the underbelly of a plane
to get out of cuba. his body fought
to keep warm in the frigid reaches.
most hearts would have stopped, but his
pumped his arteries all those cold miles, saying
go on, go on. saying *i'll do this work
now,* undaunted by tomorrow.

in my yard, a birdhouse sat
atop a pole. a pair of chickadees
squeezed their plump bodies in and out
of the small hole. one afternoon,
we found the birdhouse lying on the ground.
with no nest in sight, my husband
propped it on the base. a few days later,
it fell again. this time, a small rectangular nest
sat upright in the grass. inside: four
speckled eggs scarcely larger
than jellybeans. this time, after setting
the nest in place, we tied the house back on.

every day since, i've looked for the chickadees,
thinking how the body of the female used
every whit of excess vitamins and protein,
of high-strung bird energy wrested from flying
and seed-gathering to form the tiny eggs

her magnum stretched to accommodate.
meanwhile, she and her mate
gathered and pulled wisps of straw,
moss, and dry plant stems to thread
together a shelter. at last, her vagina squeezed
out the eggs and her whole body
vigorously warmed them—all on a chance,
the same thin chance we all reach for

The Common Grackle

A fluffy grey chick stranded below high
acidic cedar shrubs. We near. It tries
to fly. And flies—a foot or two. The wings
reveal—in stretching—pink inside each edge.
A leg in landing crumples. What is there
but hope? I ask what you—my out-of-town
friend—think about our taking it to a
rehab center. I hold it in a hand—
soft, bony, it makes small efforts to get
away. My fingers tighten. Later, we
are told they put it down. The fractures too
severe, damaged muscle. Dehydration.
A life that I'd once held. I'd picked it up
and seen its parent swoop. Nothing but hope.

newts in amplexus

underwater, the male held
the female's neck with his back legs
as though sitting on her head.

the pair were almost
completely still. every ten
minutes, he rippled his tail

and pheremones waved
over her. halfway through,
a second male tried to

wedge between them,
then gave up. but soon a dog–
running, barking–tromped

the pond. in dirt-blurred water,
the male unclasped, watched the female
rise to the surface.

The Birdbath

In my dream, the birds were using
the new heated birdbath, not frolicking
but happy tweets and light
jittery movement–the cardinal
with his shining eye, a handful
of chickadees, those diligent house-
holders banded together for winter.

In life, it stands near the feeder,
a cast-iron, scalloped, almost heart-shaped cup,
and waits—tethered, steaming, empty.

nature essay

did you know, if you have a yard
in the right climate, it's probably patrolled
by one male hummingbird? like the god
who knows every hair on your head,
this bird has memorized each flower
in your yard, including the precise times
at which their nectar cups fill up.

in this way, he can manage
his realm (and his sugar fixes)
efficiently. when he's not busy drinking,
he catches insects and defends your yard
against intruder hummingbirds.
so, if, like most americans, you harbor
many secret fears, one of which is being
overrun, you can delete that one.

female hummingbirds, by contrast,
tend to lay low so as not to rile
their touchy counterparts. their reasons
to survive are bigger than whatever charge
they'd get from gorging on nectar cups.

many different conclusions could be drawn.
for one, it seems clear that the image
of the hummer with its long beak buried
in a trumpet-like flower is indeed phallic.
another is that, for the benefit of survival,
it is sometimes necessary to weigh

the costs of pleasure carefully. finally,
you might apprehend that you do not really
own your property: some hummingbird probably
has an equally valid claim and knows it more intimately.

"blue"

if i said bluebirds and steller's jays are not really blue,
that blueness is a trick their feathers are engineered
to reflect, would this mean anything
to you? as if other blueness were a state of being
separate from perception—or is it? if feathers look blue
doesn't that make the bird blue—or blue enough—or are we
to test blue objectively to make sure it's real, and, since birds
have been tested and fail, the whole avian kin-dom
may lay no claim to blue? this raises questions
i am not equipped to answer. for example—
my chinese friend who passes as a tribal member isn't
indian because she passes, so maybe birds
aren't blue no matter how they are perceived or perceive each other.
or what about that study on race in brazil where white-
identifying people were found to have more african ancestry
than black-identifying people, so maybe feeling blue
is the operative question, but the trouble is we can ask and ask
away and the birds will never tell us. it's also possible
that being blue in brazil means something different
than being blue in the u.s. or is blueness determined by who's
asking the question so that i can foist my conception
on birds throughout the world? but if i couldn't base the question
on my own conception, then i could only ever answer
a fragment of the question, which may be true after all.

and if the categorizers were to decide that blue can no longer
apply to feathers, wouldn't bluebirds and blue jays
be forced to change the names they don't know they have,
not to mention great blue herons who don't look blue

anyway, except when afternoon lights up their ruffed
grey, rendering them too rich and illuminating to settle quietly
under the non-color of granite, rainydays, raccoons,
squirrels, and ash, all too flat to accommodate
the majestic heron who instead was bestowed with the honorary
but unachievable blue designation only to lose it most likely
in very short order? and what about warner brothers' roadrunner
who's drawn blue though real roadrunners are brown streaked in black
(save some blue skin near the eye)? could it be that the cartoon
roadrunner, that unpreyable prey, that table-turning phoenix,
is the only truly blue bird, the one real mccoy,
the post hoc archetype that all other "blue" aves
unknowingly aspire to as they fly off into equally unblue skies?

beleaguered oases

i.
sometimes passing through desert, i'm startled by lakes
like Tule and Indian Tom, along California's top edge.
white pelicans float like sturdy, self-contained steamers,
yellow-headed blackbirds call from wide-legged stances on shore-
      rocks,
also redwings, gadwalls, and canada geese with fuzzy, near-grown
      children in tow
congregate in these oases ringed by slim layers of cattails and lush
      marsh grass,
then huge swaths of sage brush set up against dusty buttes
that only up close show patches of dry grass
breaking up their sand-dune smoothness. now and then a bright,
      sprinkler-fed
field dots the land, sometimes stacked with alfalfa.

coming upon each lake
the heart lightens, letting go of some tension it was carrying,
secretly perhaps, having feared the dry landscape
(or maybe it rides the arc of bird-sound–
duck murmurs and blackbird songs like bagpipe notes
mixing with the ck-calls
of terns and grebes to stew
an ecstatic cacophony
something like a jungle must be).
but there's a way too
in which tenuousness and rarity
sharpen beauty, bring our blurry
distracted glimpses into focus.

ii.
down Hill Road, across from Tule Lake, farmers
flank their houses with signs–
simple black on white, letters rough—
"Honor your Oath, People Before fish," "A New
Endangered Species: Tule Lake Farmers," and set against a tractor,
        writ large,
"Adoption: A Life Without Regret."

as with any colonists, one can say
they don't belong, but what of
these homesteading families
who poured generations of effort
into drawing horseradish or potatoes
out of alkaline soil
at the urging of a government
that saw desert as waste?
once a bankrupt policy enroots itself
in successive generations
of stauntons and schaffners,
through decades of early morning labor
and isolated roadless winters (or the more daring
and desperate winter drives along train tracks),
can logic still hold forth
about the quixotry of farming desert,
about how endangered lost river suckers
need the irrigation water because it fuels
the marsh that shelters them from pelicans
or how some of the last colonies
of those same pelicans
will desert their young
if farmers drain their nesting grounds, opening

their brooding and rearing to coyotes?
tell me we can overcome the tragedy
that no home feels as real as our own.

loving badly

"anything worth doing is worth doing badly."
                    –Jack Gilbert

sometimes i think of the strange curse
of being anathema to what i love perhaps most of all
though love of course is hard to measure—sometimes
seeming to be all or nothing and other times
as though it may be possible to love only certain qualities
of a thing or a person or even to love something a little
like a flavor of ice cream that has to catch you
at the right moment—but nature, especially
its animals, is one of those things i love
without condition, occasionally even thinking
that death through some natural force
might be the least regrettable type. so it's terrible
that almost every step i take
harms nature or incites its fear.   i could point to the clothes i buy,
the damage wrought by dyes and
bleaches or the creation and persistence of synthetic fabric. or
            driving a car,
the emissions being only a small part of it.   also oil and gas
drip onto the road without my knowing it,
then mix with rain and finally slide into my favorite bay
to be absorbed first by plankton, then to proceed
all the way up the food chain. or the produce i eat—
genetically engineered and laden with pesticide.
or my soles' carrying invasive seeds
into distant wildlife refuges. of most of this
i know almost nothing, especially not the specifics
that would require me to change my life probably beyond
            recognition.

but walking among the animals tells of my undesirability differently.
herons measure my approach, willing to tolerate up to a few feet
before squawking into loping flight, while ducks on a lake
waste no time skidding into air if webbed toes
won't paddle fast enough to escape the crunch of feet
too big to creep. even the self-absorbed deer nosing bushes
jumps into a run so fast all four hooves lift
when it catches sight of me. because their fear
often saves them i'm grateful, but, at the same time, lonely.

rumination

my friend says cows are too dumb
to understand quality of life. she thinks the fact
that they used to wander on grass
in our little town, but now are caged
on concrete is sad only to her. the slow wearing down
of their bones is a subject they do not contemplate.
but i think you can be miserable and not know
it's called that. and now i'm beginning to wonder
if the idea of there being no sorrow without joy—
the two inexorably linked—is wrong too.
isn't it sorrow if a body hones itself for millions
of years to wander through fields, chewing
and digesting, then is shanghaied to a world
where there is barely room to move
and three of its four stomachs lie fallow?
knowing a lack as a lack paves
a way to talk about it.
but the things we never say are real too.
and the things we don't know to say,
do our limitations diminish them?

stages of night

if you walk the slough at sunset, you might see
a group of green-winged teal floating along
murmuring.

but you'll miss the male's velvety brown head,
his emerald-swashed eyes. likewise, twilight blurs
ermine spots in a russet breast, herring-
bone sides fog-and-rain grey.

later, the shoulder's white stripe, the rump's pale
triangle, his small size and dark head will let you sift
out of a book what must have been.

as if you saw teal shadows.   lack of light
intervened to fade magnificence.   through a glass darkly
as explained the apostle paul. and yet and yet
it's a story you can tell, the small congregation

floating in life's happy raft, whatever it is about
ducks that imparts happiness—calm unperturbed
quacks, apparent aimlessness on water,
an amused look in so many eyes—

it's there, you feel it, though dark feathers
obscure it and–all around–night encroaches.   at last
you tear yourself away and walk on.   a hawk calls from
a fence post, back turned, seemingly endless

keening, the same stretched, perfect note.
and thinking hawk? owl? hawk? owl?
trying to ignore the slenderness of the head,
you walk into the final minutes of light,

the last duck you see simply brown, solitary,
searching the same patch of water repetitively
until your head turns too quickly   and this time
you know poring over a bird book won't sort out

what you saw, the gloaming at last
too steep, and so you are left with that
solitary searching that fills your own small soul.

let me tell you about the snakes

who threaded the stone wall like a needle
like a grandmother's knitting.
three slender ropes, each
a foot long, young but bigger than newborns.
it was early spring the way it is in so many
poems, in so many unexpected pleasures.
they'd probably just emerged from the den.
two black with yellow stripes down the sides,
yellow bellies, one orange and black
with similar markings. they sunned
themselves there on the wall
by the shoulderless highway. hold your breath
with me and hope for them. they looped through
holes in old mortar (*been there since*
the fifties, said the farmer who stopped his truck to look).
they rested on top of each other and under
each other, they seemed to move effortlessly.
they smelled the world with the flick of a tongue
and were not afraid. their heads ticked
back and forth like the pendulum on a clock.
to get close, i sat on the wall. they stayed
five minutes with me, retreating
when the farmer arrived. that morning, i thought
i'd woken to a day like any other.

swimming through history

i. *the truckee and the skagit*

ankle-deep in summertime, the truckee
lets you climb down and taste it,
but the wide, deep skagit
demands a firmer commitment.

ii. *learning the skagit*

at home, when i'm getting more
than a glimpse through a car window,
i'm walking the dike
above the skagit, kingly or queenly,
the way dutch farmers devised it.
glancing, these downstream waters
look still as a painting, linger in one spot,
yet the whole mass rushes.

but once, upstream in early
december, i watched the last chum
undulate in slow motion, their bodies
ripped by so many rocks
in their against-current trek
that blood streaked them. only
a few swam; the rest floated. the sight
made the toil of sisyphus

look easy. another time, i saw the tiny
nearly finless body of a juvenile

barely larger than a tadpole, stranded
on the beach at deception pass.
the silver body throbbed at the gill
while the oversized eye stared upward.
when i cupped the fingerling in my hands
to throw it back to sea, it flopped
down to escape me.

still, all my looking makes
just a drop next to the hours
i sit and write brief after brief
to keep more water in the banks
during the months when the skagit
is lowest or negotiate day in,
day out for salmon to have more water
to spawn and rear in, only to find myself
lost and cut off. i long to squish
my fingers and toes in mud or throw
my body headlong into current.
what wisdoms and strengths would the river
feed me if i could let myself go?
but how to face the great surge of life,
bearing effort that may come to nothing?

iii. *visiting the truckee*

yesterday, remembering all this, i climbed
down to the truckee. here and there, logs made
crevices where adult fish could build redds.
i lay on a rock and let the river tug my feet
feeling how easily it could crush my unnimble
body on the rocks. i peered at the little pools
along the sides of the banks, and saw how the sun

shining through slower ripples
made a pulsing snakeskin pattern. i thought of the newly
hatched fry who might shelter there

except that—thanks to the dam and other
interference—the lahontan cutthroat
who ruled these reaches were killed off
more than sixty years ago.
now, stocked trout and ghosts swim here.

late fall, Skagit chum run

salmon know there is
something more important
than their own lives. upstream
a few sluggish bodies
flicker in their last
arcs. eyeing heaven and hell,
the rest float—pummeled, broken
through realization.

falling and alighting

the reader's innocence

one day you sat reading, innocently reading–
was it you or i?—are you and i interchangeable? i confess
it was me who sat reading—as innocent as i can ever claim to be—
a poem about honeysuckle by brigit pegeen kelly,
and this poem brought the term "catherine wheel" into my vocabulary
so that now the honeysuckle has been obliterated and
crushed limbs impaled on spikes, slow bloody death
and the cheers that were said to accompany it
occupy my thoughts or flash in like those 30-second newscasts
on otherwise quiet moments. was i who chose to read this,
not knowing what it held, deprived of anything?
or is that what poetry strives for—always the unexpected?
i didn't know the poem was about honeysuckle
when i started. it had a german title that i meant to look up
but haven't, so much of letters just out of reach even
with my good education. but one of the things about agonizing
intentional deaths is that they are never out of reach, everyone
understands the fact of them and tries to imagine
what it would be like. it's only the why of them that escapes some
but perhaps not everyone. in this way they may be better subjects
than honeysuckle, which does little for me unless i imagine
plucking the flower, biting off its tender base, sucking nectar
that the vine never meant for me to taste.

urban relations

i.
a few weeks after arriving in san diego,
on my way to the car from the atm,
bundle of flannel? man? falling from a 4th story
window, then the sound, somewhere between a slap—
like the slap of a body on a pool after jumping inexpertly
from a high board—and a thud. then the seep of a man's head—

crimson puddle inching from sidewalk to street. head
turned sidewards as if taking one last look,
but brown eyes blank now. on the face of the suicide
nothing is written, and jumping looks like falling.
this is what i learned that sunny afternoon.

ii.
6 weeks later, my neighbor shoots up
early Saturday outside my window.
the cat excitedly looks out.
it's the neighbor who chit chats in a stiff voice,
who is often outside lounging in the courtyard
in the afternoon. hiding from his girlfriend
his habit, he stands facing outward,
arm bent, green plastic syringe handle pointing out of his shoulder
towards me. trees block the view from his balcony
so this moment has been gifted me.

iii.
i remember working on the reservation, the emails week after week
about funerals, my despair at the loss of people i barely knew,

but the loss was different, mediated somehow.
once the cultural resources worker explained to the county coroner
who was sometimes notified of ancient skeletons coming unburied
or being accidentally dug up: *even if the dead aren't Indian,*
we bury them like they're our own father or mother. here
by the beautiful beaches, subtractions happen differently.

holiday remembrance

come christmas, the
indian tribe gets flowers
from a funeral parlor—
a thank you for the dying
that's over and done,
a nod to deaths still to come.

Rescue

In Japan, ten thousand dead from an earthquake and tsunami,
radiation levels 1,250 times normal. In Lybia, bombs fall
in some way from my own hand. My mind takes refuge in the boy,
17, who jumped off the Golden Gate Bridge
during a field trip and survived. I don't know the boy, who'd earned
    the nickname
"Otter" and jumped from the Lake Sonoma Bridge
before derailing his classmates' museum excursion.
Still I think I can understand his ordinary pain,
his making himself a spectacle to share for a moment
how it hurts to live. I remember biking recklessly
through traffic jams around that age, internally daring death
when a driver screamed *Do you want to die?*
and once, after walking miles in below-zero weather,
almost taking a ride
from a stranger whose painted-over commercial van
was plastered inside with pin-ups. I hoisted myself onto that van
    step
only to step down after walls stared back. The driver laughed
when I said I'd changed my mind. Back then, my life was a
    currency
I might be willing, on a given day, to throw away or trade.
True, I am not that boy, whose muscular, 5'2" frame saved him
according to the 50-something father
who rescued him while surfing.
No one knows much about the boy—a recent transfer to his
    school—
but, in my mind, I can hear the surfer ask
Are you alright? and the boy respond *No, not really.*

The purity of it comforts me, and I like to imagine the boy
alighting in an adulthood
where bridges don't call out to him, or, if they do, he walks right on
        by.
It's something small that I know is possible, so I hurl it up
like an anchor to the sky.

Acknowledgements

Thanks to the editors of the following publications, in which these poems first appeared:

Altered Scale: "Interior Architecture" and "urban relations"

Anon: "newts in amplexus"

Avocet: "stages of night"

Awakenings Review: "half-life," "eggshells," and "fracture"

Beleaguered Oases: "beleaguered oases" and "let me tell you about the snakes"

Bared (2016): "beholden"

bi magazine: "word games" and "life without descartes"

Bisexuality and Transgenderism: InterSEXions of the Others (Jonathan Alexander and Karen Yescavage eds. 2004): "Outing"

Clackamas Literary Review: "taking stock"

Crab Creek Review: "Rescue" and "a few remaining trees"

Fire on her Tongue: An Anthology of Contemporary Women's Poetry (2014): "'blue'" and "the reader's innocence"

Gertrude: "paean for the body" and "stain" (published under the title "ink")

Harrington Lesbian Literary Quarterly: "If," "appointment," "porous landscape," "dirt under the fingernails," "bulkheads," "somersault," and "fungus"

Knock Journal: "rumination"

Lavender Review: "swimming through history"

Push! Magazine: "Small Town Vignettes"

Sinister Wisdom: "mainland fantasy"

Swell: "The Full Pulse of Happiness," "Home Remedies," and "kilter"

The San Diego Poetry Annual 2012-13: "terror"

Thank you to Manny for his incredible support and understanding.

And to Squaw Valley Community of Writers and all the poets I've met and learned from throughout my time there.

And to the poets at Hamline University, especially Deborah Keenan, Katrina Vandenberg, and Juliet Patterson.

And to Carol Guess, Claudia Poquoc, Jill Grunewald, Mary Kasimor, Scot Siegel, Diana Fisher, and Laurie Posner.

And to my writer's group in the Skagit Valley, which still lives on in my imagination.

And to Risa Denenberg, Mary Meriam, and Rita Mae Reese of Headmistress Press.

And to Gordon Henry, Kelli Russell Agodon, and the late Rane Arroyo all of whom encouraged me at moments when it was sorely needed.

And to my dear friends Karen, George, and Cindy—artists who inspired and supported my work for the many years leading up to this book.

And to Jasmine Gonzales Rose, Steve Macias, and Toni Thomas.

And to Bob Hass—a tremendous teacher whose graduate poetry writing class I was lucky beyond words to sneak into during law school.

And to Anna Bergman for offering me my first reading.

And to Jim Elkins for indefatigably supporting and promoting the creative work of lawyer-poets, including my own.

And to D.A. Powell and again to Katrina and Carol for their unbelievably generous blurbs.

And to Zachary for endless distraction and inspiration, none of which I could have lived without.

About the Author

Ann Tweedy's first chapbook, *Beleaguered Oases,* was published by tcCreativePress in 2010, and her second chapbook, *White Out,* was published by Green Fuse Press in June 2013. Her poetry has appeared in *Clackamas Literary Review, Rattle, damselfly press, Lavender Review, literary mama, Harrington Lesbian Literary Quarterly,* and elsewhere. Ann is currently a student in Hamline University's Master of Fine Arts Program. Originally from Southeastern Massachusetts, she has lived in many places on the West Coast and in the Midwest and now makes her home in Washington State. In addition to writing poetry and essays, she is a law professor and a practicing attorney who represents Indian Tribes.

CPSIA information can be obtained
at www.ICGtesting.com
Printed in the USA
LVOW13s2340160317
527541LV00006B/174/P